W9-AUQ-224

Native
Americans

Written by Sean Sheehan
Illustrated by David McAllister

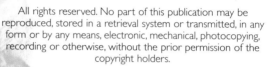

This is a Parragon Publishing Book
This edition published in 2003

Parragon Publishing
Queen Street House
4 Queen Street
Bath BA1 1HE, UK

Copyright © Parragon 2000

ISBN 0-75259-873-2

Printed in China.

Produced by
Monkey Puzzle Media Ltd

Contents

Who left behind only their burial mounds?

The Hopewell people lived in the valleys of Ohio and Illinois for 1,500 years from 800 B.C. The little that is known about their culture comes from objects found in their burial mounds. These mounds reached over 30 ft (10 m) in height, and as much as 200 ft (70 m) around.

Who first discovered America?

Pottery, stone ornaments, and clay images have been found in Hopewell burial mounds.

Many thousands of years before Christopher Columbus sailed

across the Atlantic from Europe, people trekked into North America across a land bridge from Siberia. This happened some 10 to 12,000 years ago, when the Ice Age was coming to an end. Some historians also believe that people might have been living in South America over 30,000 years ago. Some of these people may have moved north into the southwestern United States.

Why were Native Americans called "Indians"?

Before America was known to Europeans, the explorer Christopher Columbus planned to travel around the world and reach India by sailing west. After a journey lasting over two months, he finally reached land—probably the Bahamas—and thinking he had reached India, called the people there Indians! The name stuck and became a label for all the different Native Americans living in the New World.

Columbus meets non Europeans in the New World.

Who had a good government before the Europeans?

Five tribes, former enemies, came together and formed the Iroquois Confederacy in the early 1600s. Decisions were made by a council who were all men and elected for life, but women had the right to fire any councillor.

Cornplanter, an Iroquois chief.

How many Native Americans lived in America before Europeans arrived?

Impossible to know for sure. Some historians estimate under 1.5 million Native Americans. But others say these numbers are ridiculously low for such a vast land mass. They give figures of between 8 and 18 million.

Whose name means "those who have vanished?"

The Hohokam people, who lived in the Arizona desert, near the border with Mexico, over 2,000 years ago. They survived by building canals and farming. They were given their name by the Pima people who later came into the region where "those who have vanished" once lived.

Who were the Mogollon and the Mimbres?

The Hohokam are not the only Native Americans who have vanished from the southwestern United States. The Mogollon people lived in the mountains on the Arizona—New Mexico border. The Mimbres also lived in this region, but by around 1300, like the Mogollon, they were extinct.

What started at 4 a.m. in 1607?

The first permanent English settlement in the United States. One settler said "About foure in the morning, wee descried the Land of Virginia." And the settler went on to exclaim how they: "...got good store of Mussels and Oysters, which lay upon the ground as thicke as stones."

Who was inspired by the Iroquois government?

Benjamin Franklin, co-author of the Constitution. He thought the idea of a government like the Iroquois Confederacy could be used by the English colonies. The eagle on the United States shield is the Iroquois bald eagle—also a symbol for the Iroqouis nation.

Where did Native Americans get their horses?

FOR A LONG TIME, IT WAS THOUGHT THERE WERE NO HORSES IN NORTH AMERICA until the Spanish brought them in the 1550s. But fossil records show evidence of horses long before Europeans arrived. At some unknown date they disappeared, only to be reintroduced by the Spanish.

Was there really a Sioux tribe?

No. The word Sioux was adopted by French explorers who picked it up from the Chippewa tribe. Sioux is a Chippewa word for "enemy." The Chippewa used it to describe the Lakota people, whom they had pushed westward from the Western Great Lakes, where the Lakota originally lived. So the Sioux are really the Lakota, a name that means "where the people of peace dwell."

Which tribes hunted buffalo?

The Blackfeet, Cheyenne, Comanche, Crow, and Lakota people all lived on the Great Plains, a large area stretching from the Mississippi River to the Rocky Mountains and from Canada to Texas. Although they had important differences, they lived by hunting herds of buffalo on the prairies.

Who were the five civilized tribes?

THE CHOCTAW, CHEROKEE, CREEK, CHICKSAW, AND SEMINOLE TRIBES, living in the Southeast of North America, were called the "Five Civilized Tribes" by early white settlers. They were given this name because of similarities between their cultures and those of the Europeans. The tribes lived in planned villages, were farmers as well as hunters, and some were wealthy enough to own slaves. Later, some of them became Christians and adopted other aspects of the settlers' lives.

Which tribe worked together as one large family?

The Creek divided their land into family plots, but the work of farming was carried out by all of them working together as equals, including their chief. Some of the harvest was stored in a special building and shared for public occasions.

Osceola was the leader of the Seminole people of what is now Florida and Georgia.

A Mandan village by the bank of the Missouri.

What is special about the Seminole of Florida?

They are a mixed group, formed from the survivors of various Florida tribes after the European slave trade had almost wiped them out. Mostly Creek, they were joined by runaway black slaves and successfully resisted attempts to root them out from the swampland.

What tribe believe the number seven to be sacred?

The Cherokee hold seven ritual ceremonies, six of which took place annually and the seventh every seven years. They had seven "mother towns," originally the headquarters of their seven clans.

Which tribe hunted and farmed by the Missouri River in North Dakota?

The Mandans hunted the buffalo like other Plains people, but they also lived in permanent villages built high up on the banks of the Missouri. They farmed the land and grew maize. The explorers Lewis and Clark spent a winter living with the Mandans before heading west.

Where did the Apache come from?

THEY CAME FROM NORTHWESTERN CANADA WHERE THEY HAD LIVED as hunters and where farming was impossible. Their migration to the Southwest began around A.D.1000 and continued over the next 500 years.

Which western state is named after a tribe?

Utah is named after the Utes, a people who lived on the edge of the Plains and the Great Basin. Oklahoma comes from "okla homma," which means "home of the red people."

Which tribe helped two Americans explore west of the Mississippi?

President Thomas Jefferson invited Lewis and Clark to explore this unknown land. With the help of the Nez Perce people, who built canoes for them and drew maps of the rivers, they succeeded in reaching the Pacific.

Who had tails on their boats?

The Mandan people built the frame of a one-person boat out of willow branches and covered it with buffalo hide. They left the buffalo's tail on the hide and attached a piece of wood to it, so the boat had a built-in rudder.

Who hunted with duck decoys?

In northwestern Nevada hunters made decoy ducks out of grasses and plant stalks. They floated them on lakes and marshes within bow-shooting distance of the hunter's hide. Migrating birds, deceived into thinking it was safe to land, became sitting ducks for the hunters' arrows!

Who could not live without the birch?

Tribes who lived in the northeast of North America used the wood of birch trees for building their wigwams and canoes. The bark of the birch was tough and weatherproof, so they used it for making baskets and storage vessels.

Many Native American tribes could not have survived without horses.

What sport had up to 200 players?

PEOPLE OF THE SOUTHEAST, ESPECIALLY THE CHOCTAW, WERE FANATICAL players of a stick-and-ball game played with large teams. French settlers thought the stick looked like a bishop's crosier. So when they introduced it to Europe, they called it La Crosse, hence the game known today as lacrosse.

Who liked giving things away?

Better-off families of Pacific coast tribes demonstrated their wealth by holding potlatch ceremonies and handing out gifts to their guests, which could number over 100. The worth of a gift depended on the status of the guest. The hosts expected to get back the worth of their gifts by being invited to potlatches held by their guests. Although potlatches became illegal in the 1900s, they still take place today.

Who hunted for heavyweight prey?

The Plains people lived by hunting the mighty buffalo. It was about 6 ft (2 m) high, and despite its tremendous weight 1 ton (1,000 kg), could still run very fast in a stampede. Before horses were used, Plains hunters tried to sneak up on buffalo downwind, disguised in animal skins. Another extremely dangerous technique was to stampede the buffalo over cliffs or into pens. On horseback, the buffalo was brought down with spears, and bows and arrows tipped with iron or stone. Bows were specially strengthened and shortened to under 3 ft (1 m) for easier use on horseback.

How did Native Americans record history?

They painted a record of past events in picture-writing and symbols on animal hides. They also passed stories on by word-of-mouth. Many people memorized the tribe's history to pass it on to the next generation.

How valuable were eagle feathers?

Around 1850, a valuable horse could be exchanged for 15 eagle feathers. Their value came from their scarcity and religious importance. Especially valuable were the more colorful feathers of young eagles that took a long time to capture. Prized feathers decorated headdresses and costumes.

Did the tribes trade with one another?

Yes, at fixed times of the year tribes came together at special meeting places to trade. Nomadic people from the Plains with surplus buffalo skins would trade them for farm produce from settled tribes.

Who did not bury the dead?

SOME OF THE PLAINS TRIBES CONSTRUCTED scaffolding, or used trees, to hold the body above ground, safe from wild animals while it decayed. The Huron people placed the body in a coffin and kept it above the ground on poles for up to 12 years before the bones were buried.

Possessions, like this warrior's headdress and feathers, were left close to the corpse.

The apartments of the Pueblo tribes.

Who lived in longhouses?

Iroquois tribes lived in groups of up to 100 people in long and narrow houses. These houses were about 25 ft (7.5 m) wide and 150 ft (45 m) long, built using wooden poles covered with strips of tree bark. Platforms added to the walls indoors were used as beds and benches, and the earthen floors were covered with more bark or woven mats. Partitions divided one family area from another, but "neighbors" sometimes shared a cooking fire.

Who welcomed the morning Sun from the rooftops?

The Mandans lived in domed timber lodges with layers of grass and sods of earth on the rafters. Such a sturdy structure could easily support the weight of the village elders, who had a tradition of climbing on the rooftops at dawn to greet each day.

Did the Native Americans have toothbrushes and hairbrushes?

Of course! Porcupine hairs were used for bristles and sometimes a stick was cut into the right shape and frayed at the edges to make a toothbrush. The tail of a porcupine was cut and crafted to make a hairbrush.

Who were the first Americans to live in "apartments"?

SOME 700 YEARS AGO, THE ANASAZI PEOPLE STARTED BUILDING apartmentlike blocks out of adobe (unburned, sun-dried bricks). The apartments rose up in canyons and at the entrances to caves in Arizona and New Mexico. Ruins of one large site, Pueblo Bonito, show that well over 1,000 people lived here. In the 1500s, Pueblo tribes also built rows of adobe houses up to five stories high. They reached the upper stories by climbing connecting ladders. Native Americans still live in some of these adobe houses.

Who lived in thatched houses?

The Choctaw people, who lived in the semitropical climate of the Southeast. They used the leaves of the palmetto, a small palm tree, as a thatch for their houses. This allowed the air to circulate better than any wood, stone, or brick, and prevented the house from becoming uncomfortably hot inside.

What are sweat lodges?

Plains tribes used these for religious ceremonies. They were windowless and dome-shaped. Inside the lodge, a collection of large stones was set over a fire to generate heat and steam.

Two Blackfeet women with a child on a horse-drawn frame called a travois.

What is a hogan?

THE NAVAJO PEOPLE OF THE SOUTHWEST LIVED IN BEEHIVE-SHAPED HOUSES

called hogans. The frame of a hogan was built with poles of pinewood, or sometimes stone. Then the hogan was covered with a layer of dried mud. The Navajo still like to have a hogan on their land, close to their more modern house. Many still live just in hogans.

How was dried buffalo dung used inside a tepee?

It made a useful fuel for cooking and for keeping warm, because when it burned it was almost smokeless. The little smoke produced by the fire escaped through a gap at the top of the tepee created by cutting open a flap in the buffalo hide.

The inside of a tepee was warm and comfortable.

11

Spearing fish required patience and skill.

Who has boomerangs that do not come back?

The Hopi people use a curved stick, about the same size as a boomerang, to throw through the air and bring down rabbits. Hopi hunters gather in a large circle, up to a mile wide, and move forward together. When a rabbit appears, a nearby hunter throws his stick.

How was food boiled without saucepans?

Simple. A hole was dug, lined with rawhide to prevent leaking, and filled with water into which red-hot stones were dropped. The stones made the water hot enough to boil meat, with more stones from the fire being added as necessary.

What did the Navajo learn from the Spanish?

The Navajo used to be nomadic hunters, but they learned about farming crops and sheep from the Spanish, who arrived in the 1500s. At first, the Navajo stole sheep from the Spanish, then in time they became expert sheep farmers.

What can you find to eat in a desert?

More than you might think. The fruit of most cacti is edible. Some cactus fruit needs cooking, but the prickly pears can be eaten fresh once their thorns have been removed. Some cactus seeds can be pounded to make flour, and a number of edible roots can be dug out from underground.

What are the three sisters?

Maize, beans, and squash were called the three sisters by the Iroquois. They were so important as sources of food that they were thought of as female spirits. Maize (corn) was a valuable source of carbohydrate, beans were a source of protein, and squash provided important vitamins. European settlers learned to grow pumpkins from Native Americans, and made it into one of their traditional foods for Thanksgiving—sweet pumpkin pie.

How do you keep antelope meat?

The meat of deer, antelope, turkey, and rabbit could be dried in the sun. Salt was then added as a preservative. Salt was collected from salt springs by boiling away the water, or by scraping it from a salt bed.

What was pemmican?

Pemmican was buffalo meat pounded and mixed with berries and fat to produce a type of dried food. It was stored and used later when fresh food was hard to find. Pemmican was high in protein and could be stored for years if necessary.

Who ate fast food?

The people of the Great Basin, like the Shoshone and the Paiute, lived in a land so arid it could not be farmed. They never stayed in the same place for very long, and as they moved around they lived off food that they dug from the ground. They ate grasshoppers and other insects, lizards, roots, seeds, and nuts. They were very close to their environment, but Europeans did not understand this and called them "Digger Indians."

Who hunted in disguise?

TRIBES LIKE THE CHEROKEE, CREEK, AND CHOCTAW, WHO DID NOT HAVE buffalo on their land, hunted deer instead. A solitary deer was tracked by a lone hunter, sometimes wearing a deer's hide as camouflage, and imitating a deer's mating call to attract his prey.

A Cherokee hunter approaches his prey— downwind of them.

Mohawk warriors were fearless and brave.

Who had wild hairstyles?
The Mohawks, one of the tribes that made up the Iroquois nation, had a distinctive hairstyle that remains popular with some people today. Another hairstyle was to keep one side of the scalp cleanly shaved while the other side was painted a bright color.

Why was the buffalo important to fashion?
Nearly everything the Native Americans wore was made of leather. Buffalo skin was first softened (tanned) by soaking it in water and rubbing it with fatty oils and the brains of the animal. Then it was stretched into shape across a wooden frame and dried. After scraping the hide with sandstone, the soft and supple leather could be cut and sewn into clothes. Buffalo killed later in the year had thicker hides that were more useful for making warm winter clothes.

Did Native American women wear perfume?

PERFUME WAS NOT USED, BUT WOMEN ON THE Plains liked to give a fresh scent to clean clothes by rubbing them with a herb called sweetgrass. Makeup was not common. Sometimes women painted the part in their hair red, but this was to show their age rather than to make them look beautiful.

Where do moccasins come from?

Moccasins came in many different styles—Apaches even wore long ones up to the knee.

M OCCASIN IS AN ALGONQUIAN WORD for the footwear made from buffalo or deer hides. The soles were made from hard, untanned skin (rawhide) while the uppers were made of soft, tanned skin. The two parts were sewed together with thread made from the sinews of the animal, and decorated with beads or colored feather quills. Moccasins were always made by women, and different tribes had their own designs.

How did the Pima and Papago keep warm in the winter?
The Pima and Papago came from the deep Southwest and needed very few clothes in the hot climate. But when the temperature dropped in the winter, they kept themselves warm by rubbing animal grease on their bare upper bodies.

Were feathers worn just for fun?
Some tribes used feathers for decorative or ritual purposes. But the elaborate eagle-feather headdress of the Lakota (Sioux), which reached from head to toe, could be worn only by a warrior who had proved his courage in battle. Eagle feathers were highly prized, because they were thought to be full of spiritual power.

Where was a roach worn?
On the head—because a roach is a headdress made from dyed animal hair attached to a narrow, flat piece of bone that fits onto the head. The most important kind of roach was decorated with one or more feathers to show victory or bravery in battle.

Who walked on yucca?
The Paiute lived in an extremely dry, semidesert environment where there were no buffalo to provide leather for moccasins. However, the fibre of the yucca, a desert plant, could be woven into moccasins that were light and comfortable for the climate.

Why was a bear claw necklace highly prized?
When was the last time you tried fighting a bear? The killing of a bear was an extremely dangerous activity, and it happened so rarely that the claws were very valuable. A bear claw necklace was a highly prized piece of jewelry.

Papooses were safe and sturdy, and nicer to look at than modern ones.

How did babies travel with their parents?
In a papoose (originally an Algonquian word). The papoose was made of soft animal skin and had a stiff backboard woven from twigs. It was tied onto the mother's back and the baby was held in a comfortable upright position, able to see its surroundings. Some papooses were made with sharp, projecting, wooden points, so if they fell off while the mother was riding a horse, the points would stick in the ground and protect the baby. Heavy padding formed a sun shield over the top of the papoose and this also protected the baby's head if it fell.

Who stopped eating turtles?
Many Native American tribes had rituals for their children before they were even born. People like the Nez Perce and the Northern Shoshone had ritual prayers for men who wanted to be fathers. Pregnant mothers had their own prayers, and followed a special diet, giving up meat and eating only fish and birds. A pregnant Iroquois woman stopped eating turtles in the hope that her baby would not grow up clumsy on land, like a turtle. In Navajo communities, women untied their braided hair, and freed animals like horses hoping to create a free passage and safe birth for the baby.

Who had to kill to become a man?

PEOPLE LIKE THE CHICKSAW, CREEK, AND CHOCTAW EXPECTED A YOUNG MAN
to become a man by wounding or killing an enemy in battle. Only after he had done this was the man granted an adult name and a party, held to celebrate the event.

How did Navajo girls celebrate growing up?

The first laugh of a child, and reaching the age of seven, were both marked with festivities. When a girl reached puberty, there was a ceremony called the Kinalda, in which she was covered in mud. The Kinalda still takes place today.

Which tribes trace their descent through their mothers?

Lots of tribes, including the Iroquois, Cherokee, Choctaw, Creek, Apalachee, Navajo, and Apache, trace their descent through the mother's side of their families. When an Apache male married, he always went to live in the home of his wife's mother.

A buffalo hunt was dangerous but the rewards were great.

What were marriages like?

A marriage among Plains tribes depended on the man being able to offer some horses as a dowry to his future father-in-law. An Iroquois man would give a present to his future wife instead, and they usually had a trial marriage before they agreed to the real thing.

How did Pueblo men prove their manhood?

Pueblo tribes organized mock battles between the young men and older men in their community. A young man had to show his courage and strength without injuring anyone, in order to be accepted as an adult.

What were dumaiyas?

AMONG THE HOPI PEOPLE, A DUMAIYA WAS A KIND of trial marriage: the woman lived with her boyfriend's family for a few days. If the family were happy with the arrangement, a more formal wedding ceremony would take place.

How did Plains men celebrate their first kill?

When a young man killed his first buffalo, he would be given the tastiest part, the tongue, as a reward. But the man was expected to decline the offer, and instead to share it out among his friends as a mark of generosity. In fact, to show his maturity, he wouldn't eat any of the first animal he killed.

17

Where is the spirit world?

Everywhere. The world of Native Americans is filled every which way with spiritual forces. The spirits are seen mostly as kindly, but sometimes as capable of harm to the human world. The spirits live in nature, and nearly everything, from a glorious eagle to a humble seed of corn, is believed to have spiritual powers. Aspects of life like illness or climate are still understood by Native Americans to be ruled by the spirits.

What are thunder pipes?

Plains tribes felt that thunder and lightning were punishments sent down on them by the spirits. They needed to get on good terms with the spirits to avoid their anger, so they got together for the ritual smoking of thunder pipes. These were colorful pipes decorated with eagle feathers and small bells.

A shaman is part doctor, psychiatrist, prophet and ghost-hunter.

What is a shaman?

SHAMANS, SOMETIMES MISTAKENLY CALLED witch-doctors, are men or women who are able to talk to the spirits and persuade them to do things. They are especially valued for their ability to heal the sick by driving out harmful spirits from the body. Shamans practice herbal medicine. They often work themselves into a trance-like state, experiencing spiritual visions.

What were masks used for?

Many tribes conducted ritual ceremonies to get in touch with the spirit world. Masks played a very important role in these ceremonies. They were designed and painted in special ways to show the spirits' nature, and help create a supernatural atmosphere.

Who made spirit dolls?

Pueblo tribes like the Hopi believed that the Kachina spirits escorted their people into life from a previous underground existence. The Hopi gave Kachina dolls to their children to teach them about the different types of spirits.

Who did the spirits command to walk backward?

Special warriors among the Lakota people were directed by spirits to lead their lives backward. They would only walk forward when they meant to go backward, and use "yes" and "no" in their opposite senses. But in battle they behaved like ordinary warriors.

Why are eagles sacred?

Eagles are admired by many tribes for their magnificence. They are thought of as messengers between the spirit world and the world of humans. Native Americans created special dances to imitate the eagle's flight.

Why is the Great Turtle important to the Iroquois?

It features in the Iroquois creation story. The Great Turtle is the supreme animal. When the world was made of only water, the turtle caught a pregnant woman who fell from the sky. The turtle dove into the deep, returned with bits of earth that fell with the woman, and helped create the world.

What were False Face societies ?

THEY WERE GROUPS OF RELIGIOUS PEOPLE LIKE SHAMANS WHO WORE SACRED masks. These masks, or false faces, were thought to draw and catch forces from the spirit world. The masks looked frightening but were worn in rituals meant to restore health to the sick.

White Buffalo was a shaman of the Blackfeet tribe.

What happened to a Cry Shed?

It was set on fire and burned down. The Cry Shed was built of earth and stood for the troubles and wishes of a community. As it went up in smoke, misfortunes were blown away on the wind and hopes and expectations carried to the spirit world.

Why did the Native Americans smoke pipes?

Pipe smoking was a social activity. Pipes were smoked at friendly gatherings with neighboring communities, and to mark important events. These might be the signing of a peace treaty between warring groups, or the arrival of an important guest. Tobacco was smoked in pipes that were sometimes specially made for the occasion.

Who was the Keeper of the Smoke?

He was the chief official at ceremonies conducted by the Papago and Pima people of Arizona. Every four years, they celebrated the bounty of another successful harvest. In their semidesert environment, the raising of crops was a matter of life and death, and the ceremony was a serious occasion.

Who enjoyed trick-or-treating?

THE IROQUOIS. THEY CELEBRATED A WINTER FESTIVAL IN WHICH small groups of teenagers were led singing and dancing around the village by an older woman. They stopped outside people's homes and waited for presents to be brought out to them.

A pipe could be smoked for peace or for war.

What was the most painful ceremony?

The Sun Dance of the Plains people involved dancers having skewers implanted in their chest muscles, and being attached by rope to the sacred cottonwood tree. In return for their pain, they hoped for a plentiful supply of buffalo to feed the community. The climax to the ceremony was a ritual dance. The uprooted cottonwood tree was painted and decorated, and some dancers hung themselves from the fork of the tree by the skewers in their chests.

What was the Green Corn ceremony?

A harvest thanksgiving ceremony that took place, and still does, among Native Americans in the Southeast and Northeast. Thirty or more people dance in pairs around a large fire, chanting ritual prayers in thanks to the spirits. Then they eat a large feast.

The ghost dance was a way of remembering the past.

Who danced the Ghost Dance?

THE GHOST DANCE WAS DEVELOPED BY FOLLOWERS of a Paiute holy man. He believed that ritual dancing would restore the old way of life enjoyed by the Native Americans before the arrival of Europeans. The dance spread to Plains tribes who did not like the way Europeans were changing their traditional life style. The dance promised the return of the buffalo and communication with the spirits of the dead. Although the Ghost Dance was peaceful, army authorities saw it as a threat and outlawed its performance.

What was the Busk?

An autumn harvest festival celebrated by the Creek, Cherokee, Choctaw, and Apalachee. It lasted four days, beginning with cleaning the village and putting out all fires. On the last day, as the climax to a communal feast, a new fire was lit to mark the start of a new farming year.

Who was the White Shell Woman?

An important Apache spirit. When a girl reached the age of marriage, a special ceremony was held for her. An adult dressed up as the White Shell woman to celebrate the girl's transition to womanhood.

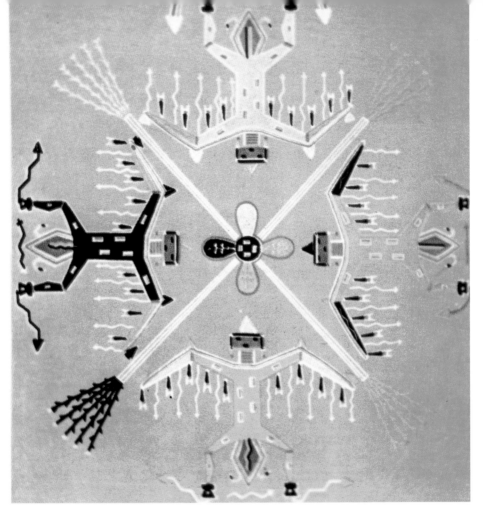

Sandpaintings have been part of Navajo ritual over many generations.

What are sand paintings?

GRAINS OF COLORED SAND ARE PAINSTAKINGLY POSITIONED TO form a complicated design of geometric shapes and symbols. Sandpaintings are a way of recording events using symbols. Today, sandpaintings are kept as works of art, but traditionally they are wiped away when the religious ritual is over.

Who made beautiful jewelry?
The Navajo became expert artistic jewelers in the 1870s. They produce fine necklaces and belts decorated with turquoise, a beautiful blue-green precious stone.

Who had beautiful battle shields?
The Crow people were famous for the care and artistry they put into their battle shields. The shields were about 2 ft (60 cm) in diameter, made of rawhide, and painted with symbols that had a personal meaning to their creator.

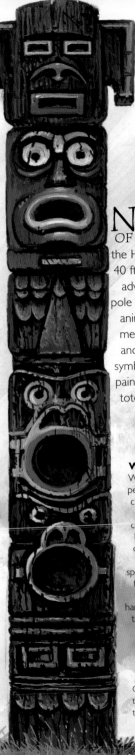

Who were, and still are, master potters?

Pueblo people like the Zuni and Hopi are the master potters of the Native American world. Centuries of experience have been passed down to today's generation of potters, who turn out beautifully-crafted and finely painted ceramics.

How do Native Americans make music?

Music is an essential part of religious, social, and military life. Logs were hollowed out to form drums of all sizes and the tops covered with tightly stretched animal skin. Turtle shells were turned into rattles, and hollowed bones made pipes that were blown in battle.

Who was kidnapped for blankets?

The Navajo began weaving blankets for their own use, but their work was so artistic that settlers in New Mexico kidnapped them and forced them to weave blankets for them. Some of these "slave blankets" are now world-famous works of art.

What do we know about the Hopewell?

The Hopewell people, who once lived in the southeastern United States, have been extinct for 500 years. Little is known about their culture. But their large burial mounds have been excavated to reveal paintings that tell the stories of complicated funeral ceremonies.

Who is a famous Tlingit?

Larry McNeil is a Tlingit from Alaska, famous for his photography and his work as a professor at the Institute of American Indian Arts in Santa Fé. He became a photographer after realizing that Alaskan Native Americans were not fairly represented in art.

What are totem poles?

NATIVE AMERICANS OF THE NORTHWEST, LIKE the Haida, built totem poles as tall as 40 ft (12 m) outside their homes to advertise their family's status. The pole would usually be in the image of animals or birds that had a special meaning for the family clan and its ancestors. Each family had its own symbols and designs, and these were painted or etched onto the wooden totem pole. Totem poles were also erected as a memorial to a deceased ancestor.

Who were the greatest tattooists?

Without a doubt, they were the Timucua people of Florida. The Timucua wore little clothing because of the hot climate. This allowed them to tattoo amazingly complicated patterns over most of their bodies. Both men and woman liked to decorate their bodies with tattoos. The Mojave people of northern California specialized in facial tattooing to show their family status, while Osage women liked tattooing spiders on the backs of their hands. People on the northwest coast used tattooing to record their family's history.

Christians mistakenly thought that totem poles were statues to gods.

23

Government forces were sometimes defeated by Native Americans.

How could a warrior achieve great honor?
Warriors of most Plains tribes thought that being able to touch an enemy during a raid, without being touched in return, was a great honor. This act, known as a coup, was regarded more highly than actually injuring the enemy or even being able to steal their horses. Some warriors went to battle carrying a "coup stick" solely for this purpose. The Blackfeet preferred to try and capture an enemy shield.

What happened at the Little Big Horn?
The U.S. Army was defeated by a combined force of Lakota (Sioux), Cheyenne, and Arapaho warriors. The Native Americans were resisting government demands to move to reservations. The army planned to block off possible escape routes and divided its regiment into groups. The main group attacked a camp near the Little Big Horn River in June, 1876, without waiting for reinforcements that were on their way. Within an hour all 225 soldiers were wiped out.

Many Native American women were sharp shooters and able horsewomen.

Which tribes were almost wiped out by Kit Carson?
The Mescaleros, and then the Navajo, were attacked and rounded up by Colonel Kit Carson in the 1860s, during the Civil War. Those who were not killed were forced onto poor reservations where almost all of them died.

What weapons did Plains warriors carry?

WHEN THEY WENT ON A RAID, THEY TOOK BOWS, ARROWS, A lance, and a shield to protect them from the lances and arrows of the enemy. They might also carry a club with a sharpened stone or a spike at the end, and a sharp knife.

Who did the Native Americans call Long Hair?

Long Hair was General Custer, the officer in charge of the U.S. Army at the battle of the Little Big Horn. The name came from Custer's habit of letting his gold-colored hair grow long—though shortly before the battle he had it cut much shorter.

Were there any women warriors?

THERE CERTAINLY WERE! RUNNING EAGLE WAS A FAMOUS Blackfeet warrior woman who led others into battle. Buffalo Calf Road Woman was equally renowned among the Cheyenne. The Lakota (Sioux) and Crow also had a tradition of including female warriors in their raiding parties.

Who was the War Woman?

The Cherokee did not go to war without first holding a special meeting to discuss the matter. At this meeting the opinion of the community's women was represented by their spokesperson—and she was called the War Woman. The fate of captured enemies was also decided by Cherokee women.

Who said—"Always remember that your father never sold his country"?

Chief Joseph of the Nez Perce said this to his sons shortly before he died in 1871. A treaty robbing the tribe of their best land had been forced on his people. Chief Joseph wanted his children to know that he had never agreed to it. After his death, war broke out between the Nez Perce and government troops.

A warrior's weapons and battle regalia.

7,000 soldiers forced the Cherokee nation to march on the Trail of Tears.

Where was the Trail of Tears?

It STARTED IN GEORGIA AND ENDED IN OKLAHOMA. THE DISCOVERY OF GOLD in Georgia made the presence of Native Americans there unwelcome to the whites. In 1938, some 16,000 Cherokees were rounded up by the army and forced at the point of bayonets to trek west to new land. The trek, which lasted throughout a cold winter and covered over 4,000 miles (6,700 km), became known as the Trail of Tears. When it was over, a quarter of the Cherokee nation was dead.

Whose hearts were buried at Wounded Knee?

Men, women, and children of the Lakota (Sioux) were massacred in 1890 at Wounded Knee Creek near Pine Ridge, South Dakota. It happened after a Ghost Dance (a ritual dance wishing back the good days before the whites came) when the Lakota people who surrendered were rounded up by the army. A tense situation developed and shooting broke out. A famous book about the event is entitled *Bury My Heart At Wounded Knee*.

Which state declared that the Cherokee nation did not exist?

The state of Georgia. Georgia declared Cherokees did not exist so it could forbid them from digging for gold, which had been discovered there. Georgia also made it illegal for Native Americans to testify in court, as they were not Christians.

Who was captured only 30 miles from safety?

In an attempt to escape the U.S. Army in 1877, two Native American chiefs led their people on a 1,600-mile- (2,600 km-) trek across Idaho, Wyoming and Montana. They were Young Chief Joseph and Chief Looking Glass. They and their people were captured just before reaching safety in Canada.

Who was captured dishonorably but died honorably?

Osceola, a chief of the Seminoles in Florida, was tricked by a false flag of truce and captured. In a prison bed, he dressed in his war outfit for the last time, said farewell to the army officers and his own family, and died peacefully.

Who died while his arms were held by a fellow Native American?
Crazy Horse, who had the greatest military record of any Sioux fighting the white man, was feared by the U.S. Army, and envied by other chiefs. Arrested at the age of 37, he was bayoneted to death by a soldier, while his arms were held by the traitor Little Big Man.

Who were the last Native Americans to fight a sustained war against the U.S. Army?
The Apaches in the 1870s. They were eventually forced onto a reservation in Arizona, but armed rebellions continued until 1896. Warriors taken in the last rebellion were finally released from prison in 1913. Where they settled, the town of Apache still stands.

Who was kidnapped and brought up as a Comanche?
The mother of Quannah Parker, a leader of the Comanches, was captured as a child from a settler's community and grew up as a Comanche. She was later recaptured and returned to her white family, but she was never able to successfully adapt to their way of life.

What did Young Chief Joseph say when his people were surrounded and outnumbered by the army?
He said these famous words—"I want to have time to look for my children and see how many I can find. Maybe I shall find them among the dead. Hear me, my chiefs, I am tired; My heart is sick and sad. From where the Sun now stands, I will fight no more forever."

How did smallpox affect the Mandans?

THE MANDAN PEOPLE LIVED ON THE UPPER Missouri in North Dakota. When they first came into contact with European settlers and traders, they caught smallpox from them. They had no resistance to it, and it wiped them out—by 1837 fewer than 130 Mandan were still alive.

Native Americans fought hard to save their way of life and traditions.

Caitlin painted 470 full length paintings of Native Americans.

She was a Paiute woman, born in 1844, who learned to read and write and educated herself. She became a translator and a go-between for her own people and the government. She later wrote her own life story, telling how white people changed the Paiute way of life.

Who was the greatest Apache warrior?

Geronimo, whose first wife and three children were murdered by Mexicans, was the greatest Apache leader. Born in 1829, he led the fight against invaders of Apache land in the 1860s. He was only once caught, and that was by a trick. He boasted famously to the army—"You have never caught me shooting." He escaped captivity, but finally surrendered in 1886 and died in prison in 1909.

Who painted Native American chiefs?

G EORGE CATLIN (1796—1872) WAS A PAINTER WHO TRAVELED WEST in the 1800s. He painted unique portraits of chiefs and Native American life, including hunting for buffalo and moose. His paintings of chiefs like Osceola are world-famous.

How did Washakie help the U.S. Army?

Washakie was a Shoshone who helped establish a successful reservation for his people. Trusted by the white authorities, he encouraged the Shoshone to act as scouts for the U.S. Army. The army honored him by renaming one of their forts in Wyoming Fort Washakie.

What was Pocahontas famous for?

She was famous for pleading for the life of Captain John Smith, an English settler in Virginia captured by the Powhatan people in 1607. She was later kidnapped by the English herself, and adapted happily to a new way of life.

What did Sequoyah invent?

A written language for his Cherokee people. Sequoyah (1770—1843) realized that a written constitution and permanent records would help strengthen the position of the Cherokee people. The first Native American newspaper appeared in Cherokee in 1828.

Who was Cochise?

He was a famous and fierce chief of the Chirricahuas, an Apache tribe, who made peace with General Howard of the U.S. Army after Howard went unarmed into his camp. He stayed loyal to the terms of the treaty until he died three years later in 1874.

Did Hiawatha really exist?

Yes, HE WAS A MOHAWK WHO SUPPORTED THE FORMATION OF THE IROQUOIS Confederacy. This union of five tribes into one democratic body was the idea of the spiritual leader Deganawidah. Hiawatha was made famous in Longfellow's poem named after him

Did Sitting Bull defeat Custer?

No, Chief Sitting Bull was not even present at the battle. Battle honours belong to Gall, the Hunkpapa Sioux leader, and to Chief Crazy Horse. Sitting Bull helped to unite the tribes who fought in the battle against the army's determination to move them off their land and onto reservations. He led his people to safety in Canada when the battle was over, but the shortage of buffalo there meant they had little to eat, and in 1881 he surrendered at Fort Buford in Montana.

The battle at Little Bighorn, June 26, 1876.

Today, the Apache way of life continues in places like Arizona.

When did a president visit a Native American reservation?

IN JULY, 1999, PRESIDENT CLINTON PAID A VISIT TO THE PINE RIDGE RESERVATION in South Dakota, scene of the Wounded Knee massacre in 1890. It was the first visit by a U.S. president for 60 years.

Where can you visit the Cherokee Heritage Center?

Just outside Tahlequah in Oklahoma. Here, visitors can learn about the history and culture of the Cherokee nation, including the Trail of Tears and Sequoyah's invention of written Cherokee.

What are the words of a modern Pueblo prayer?

Hold onto what is good, even if it is a handful of earth.
Hold onto what you believe, even if it is a tree that stands alone.
Hold onto what you must do, even if it is a long way from home.

Are Native Americans becoming extinct?

Not at all, though it was once thought they would become extinct or simply marry into the rest of the United States. But did you know that Native Americans form only 1% of the U.S. population? They occupy more space in the imagination of the United States than they do land! In the 1970s, they went to court and settled important claims to do with territory. Today, their cultural traditions are stronger than at any time in the last 100 years.

Who helped build the Empire State Building?

Mohawks. It all goes back to the 1880s, when a dozen Mohawks were hired to work on the steel girders being erected to support tall buildings. By the 1930s, when many skyscrapers were being built in New York, Mohawk construction workers were well-known for their fearless ability to work at heights. The Empire State is just one of the structures they helped to build. The Mohawk tradition of high-rise building is still alive today.

Where can the "Lost Colony" be found?
In North Carolina, where a settlement was founded in the 1580s. Settlers moved in, but their supply ship was unable to return for three years, by which time the colony had vanished. A local tribe took pity on the settlers and let them live with them. Their descendants are the Lumbee people, who still live in North Carolina today.

Who never surrendered, but made peace in 1962?
The Mikasukis people fled to the swamplands of Florida over 150 years ago. From there, they continued to insist that they were at war with the United States and its army. Finally, in 1962, they signed a peace treaty.

What happened at Wounded Knee in 1973?
The American Indian Movement seized armed control of Wounded Knee for 71 days in protest against a history of ill-treatment by the whites. The leader of the protest movement later played a role in the 1992 film *The Last of the Mohicans*.

What is a Peacemaker's Court?
It is a modern revival of traditional Navajo justice. It was started in 1990, and operates in seven courtrooms in Navajo communities. Peacemakers, not judges, listen to a dispute and decide on compensation that will satisfy both sides in the argument.

Traditions such as the Pueblo Indians' Turkey Dance still live on.

Do pow-wows still happen?
POW-WOWS FIRST started among Plains people, but have now spread to the Southwest as well—they are definitely not a thing of the past. Over 1,000 pow-wows took place every year in the 1990s—they are social festivals celebrating a vibrant cultural life.

Index

AB

CDE

FGH

IJKL

MNO

PQR

STU

VWXYZ

ACKNOWLEDGEMENTS
The photographs in this book were supplied by: Camera Press 30 (Christopher Bissell), 31 (Jonathan A Meyers); Ohio Historical Society 4; Peter Newark's Pictures 5, 6, 8, 11, 12, 15, 16, 19, 21, 22, 24, 26, 28—9.